T0071051

I Share Creation

Bob Chilcott

for SATB choir and optional percussion

Vocal score

MUSIC DEPARTMENT

OXFORD
UNIVERSITY PRESS

OXFORD
UNIVERSITY PRESS

Great Clarendon Street, Oxford OX2 6DP, England
198 Madison Avenue, New York, NY10016, USA

Oxford University Press is a department of the University of Oxford.
It furthers the University's aim of excellence in research, scholarship,
and education by publishing worldwide in

Oxford New York
Auckland Bangkok Buenos Aires Cape Town Chennai
Dar es Salaam Delhi Hong Kong Istanbul Karachi Kolkata
Kuala Lumpur Madrid Melbourne Mexico City Mumbai Nairobi
São Paulo Shanghai Taipei Tokyo Toronto

Oxford is a registered trade mark of Oxford University Press
in the UK and in certain other countries

© Oxford University Press 2006

Bob Chilcott has asserted his right under the Copyright, Designs
and Patents Act, 1988, to be identified as the Composer of this Work

Database right Oxford University Press (maker)

First published 2006

All rights reserved. No part of this publication may be reproduced,
stored in a retrieval system, or transmitted, in any form or by any means,
without the prior permission in writing of Oxford University Press,
or as expressly permitted by law. Enquiries concerning reproduction
outside the scope of the above should be sent to the Music Copyright
Department, Oxford University Press, at the address above

Permission to perform this work in public (except in the course of divine worship)
should normally be obtained from the Performing Right Society Ltd. (PRS),
29/33 Berners Street, London W1T 3AB, or its affiliated Societies in each country
throughout the world, unless the owner or the occupier of the premises
being used holds a licence from the Society

Permission to make a recording must be obtained in advance
from the Mechanical-Copyright Protection Society Ltd. (MCPS),
Elgar House, 41 Streatham High Road, London SW16 1ER,
or its affiliated Societies in each country throughout the world

13

ISBN 0-19-335570-1 978-0-19-335570-5

Music and text origination by
Jeanne Roberts
Printed in Great Britain on acid-free paper by
Halstan & Co. Ltd., Amersham, Bucks.

Contents

1. When the sun rises 5

2. The Earth 10

3. The Innermost House 11

4. Come to the great world 16

Composer's note

In looking for texts that take a positive view and show respect for the environment, I was lucky to come across these short and strong poems. They all express to me a perspective that links man and nature in a way that shows humility, strength, and interdependence relative to our time.

The piece was commissioned jointly by The Reading Phoenix Choir and the National Environmental Research Council, and was first performed by the Reading Phoenix Choir at the Gala Concert of the Association of British Choral Directors in Guildford Cathedral, in August 2005.

Duration: *c.*8 minutes

Commissioned by Norman Morris and the Reading Phoenix Choir, with support from the National Environmental Research Council, and dedicated to Norman with affection.

I Share Creation

1. When the sun rises

Anon. Chinese (2500 BC)

BOB CHILCOTT

© Oxford University Press 2006

Printed in Great Britain

OXFORD UNIVERSITY PRESS, MUSIC DEPARTMENT, GREAT CLARENDON STREET, OXFORD OX2 6DP

Photocopying this copyright material is ILLEGAL.

7
dig the well from which I drink, I farm the soil that yields my food,
dig the well, farm the soil, my
dig the well, farm the soil,
9
ALTOS
mf
A.
When the
T.
f
I share cre- a - tion, Kings can do no more.
food,
B.
f
I share cre-a - tion, Kings can do no more.
SOPRANOS
12
mf
S.
the sun ri - ses, I go, I go to work, the sun goes down, I
A.
sun ri - ses, I go to work, When the sun goes down, I take my

*Keyboard reduction for rehearsal only.

22
go, I go to work, the sun goes down, I take, I take my rest, I
go, I go to work, the sun goes down, I take, I take my rest, I
work, When the sun goes down, I take my rest, I
sun ri - ses, the sun, the sun, the sun goes down, I
sun ri - ses, the sun, the sun, the sun, sun goes down, I
25
dig the well from which I drink, I farm the soil that yields my food,
dig the well from which I drink, I farm the soil that yields my food,
dig the well, the soil, that yields my
dig the well, the soil that yields my food,

27
ff
I share cre - a - tion, Kings can do no more, I share cre - a -
I share cre - a - tion, Kings can do no more, I share cre - a -
food, I share cre - a - tion, Kings can do no more, I share cre - a -
I share cre - a - tion, Kings can do no more, I share cre - a -
30
fff
- tion, Kings can do no more, I share cre - a - tion.
- tion, Kings can do no more, I share cre - a - tion.
- tion, Kings can do no more, I share cre - a - tion.
- tion, Kings can do no more, I share cre - a - tion.

attacca

2. The Earth

Chief Seattle

3. The Innermost House

Anon. Aztec

♪ = ♪
50
mf
I, the sing - er, lift them up, I, the sing - er, lift them up.
I, the sing - er, lift them up, I, the sing - er, lift them up,
I, the sing - er, lift them up, I, the sing - er, lift them up,
I, the sing - er, lift, lift them up, lift them up.
54
p
cresc.
They are scat - tered, they
They are scat - tered, scat - tered, scat - - tered,
lift them up. They are scat - tered, scat - tered, scat - - tered,
lift them up. They are scat - tered, scat - - tered,
They, they are scat - tered, scat - tered,

poco rit.
a tempo
58
f dim.
spread a - bout.
f
p
scat - tered, may wi - ther, may wi - ther, wi - ther, may wi - ther,
f
p
scat - - tered. Wi - ther, may wi - ther, wi - ther, may wi - ther,
f
scat - - tered.
poco rit.
a tempo
f
p

61
p
E - ven though on earth my flowers may wi - ther and
wi - ther, may wi - ther, wi - ther, may wi - ther, wi - ther, may wi - ther,
wi - ther, may wi - ther, wi - ther, may wi - ther, wi - ther, may wi - ther,
p
E - - - ven though my flowers may

64
mp
p dolce
cresc.
yel - low, they shall be car - ried there, they shall be
wi - ther, may wi - ther, they shall be car - - ried there, shall be
wi - ther, may wi - ther, they shall be car - - ried there, shall be
wi - ther, may wi - ther,
wi - ther, they shall be car - - ried there, shall be
68
f appass.
ff
mp
car - ried there to the in - ner - most house, the in - ner - most house of the
car - ried there, in - ner - most house, the in - ner - most house of the
car - ried there, in - ner - most house, in - ner - most house
car - ried there, in - ner - most house, in - ner - most house

72
mf
fea - thers.
bird with the gold - en fea - thers.
mf
fea - thers, fea - thers.
bird with the gold - - en fea - thers.
mp
mf
the bird, gold - - en fea - - thers.
mp
mf
the bird, gold - - en fea - - thers.
76
rit.
p
pp
Wi - ther, not wi - ther, wi - ther, not wi - ther, wi - ther, not wi - ther.
p
pp
Wi - ther, not wi - ther, wi - ther, not wi - ther, wi - ther, not wi - ther.
pp
mm
rit.
pp

for Ron Leishmann, 70 years young

4. Come to the great world

Anon. Arctic Inuit

88
f
and see - ing the sun, see - ing the sun,
and see - ing the sun, see - ing the sun,
and see - ing the sun, see - ing the
and see - ing the sun, see - ing the

93
mp
fol - low its foot - prints in the sum - mer night,
fol - low its foot - prints in the sum - mer night,
sun, fol - low its foot - prints, feel - ing the
sun, fol - low its foot - prints, feel - ing the

97
p
mp
in the sum - mer night.
There is a
in the sum - mer night.
There is a
warmth,
feel - ing the warmth.
warmth,
feel - ing the warmth.

101
fear feel - ing the cold, come to the great world.
There is a
fear feel - ing the cold, come to the great world.
There is a
mp
come to the great world.
mp
come to the great world.

105
mf
fear feel - ing the cold, come to the great world,
fear feel - ing the cold, come to the great world, and
come to the great world, and
come to the great world,

109
and see - ing the moon, see - ing the
see - ing the moon, see - ing the moon,
see - ing the moon, see - - ing, see - ing the
and see - - ing, see - ing the moon,

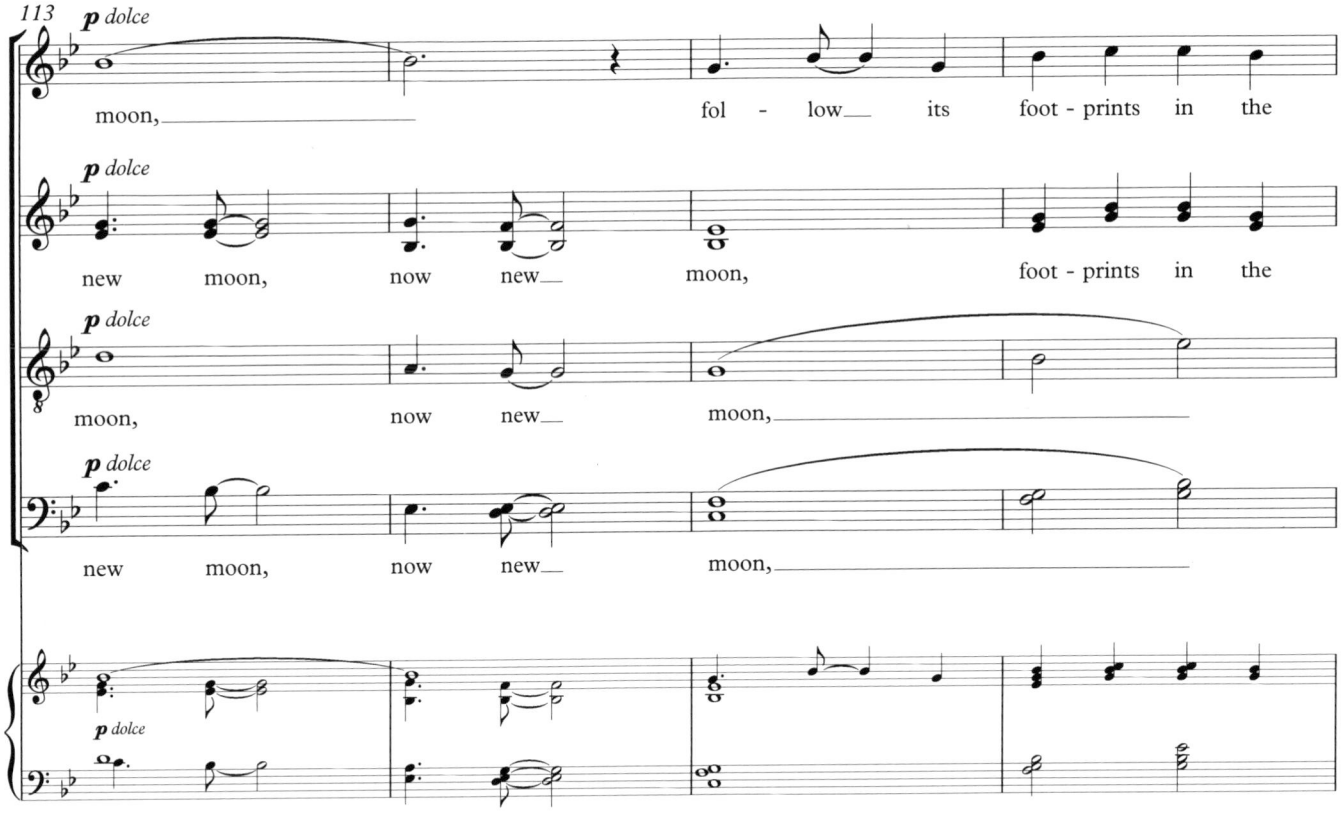
113
p dolce
moon, fol - low its foot - prints in the
p dolce
new moon, now new moon, foot - prints in the
p dolce
moon, now new moon,
p dolce
new moon, now new moon,
p dolce

117
cresc.
sum - mer night, in the sum - mer night.
cresc.
sum - mer night, in the sum - mer night.
cresc.
f
feel - ing the cold, feel - ing the cold. There is a
cresc.
f
feel - ing the cold, feel - ing the cold. There is a
cresc.
f

121
f
There is a joy, come to the great world,
f
There is a joy, come to the great world,
joy feel - ing the warmth, come to the great world. There is a
joy feel - ing the warmth, come to the great world. There is a

125
feel - ing the joy, come to the great world, and
feel - ing the joy, come to the great world, and
joy feel - ing the warmth, come to the great world,
joy feel - ing the warmth, come to the great world,

129
ff
see - ing the sun, see - ing the sun,
ff
see - ing the sun, see - ing the sun,
ff
and see - ing the sun, see - ing the
ff
and see - ing the sun, see - ing the
ff
133
mp
cresc.
fol - low its foot - prints, fol - low its
mp
cresc.
fol - low its foot - prints, fol - low its
mp
cresc.
sun, fol - low its foot - prints,
mp
cresc.
sun, fol - low its foot - prints,
mp
cresc.

137
f dim.
mp
foot - prints, fol - low its foot - prints in the sum - mer night,
foot - prints, fol - low its foot - prints in the sum - mer night,
fol - - low, fol - low its foot - prints, feel - ing the
fol - - low, fol - low its foot - prints, feel - ing the

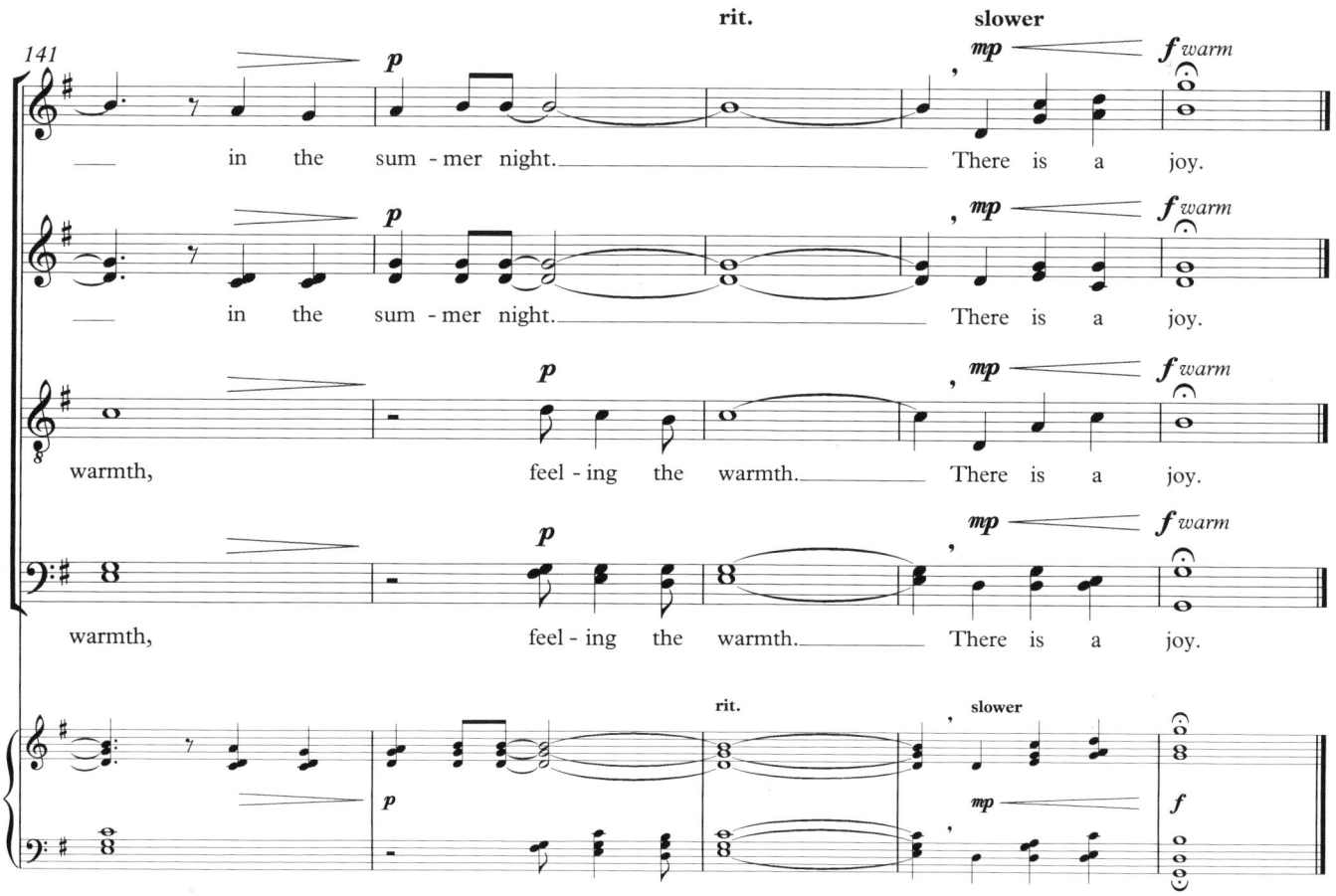
141
rit.
slower
p
mp
f warm
in the sum - mer night. There is a joy.
in the sum - mer night. There is a joy.
warmth, feel - ing the warmth. There is a joy.
warmth, feel - ing the warmth. There is a joy.
f